AUDIO ACCESS INCLUDED

PLAYBACK+
Speed • Pitch • Balance • Loop

THE BEATLES

T0056601

Cover Photo: Fiona Adams/Getty

To access audio visit:
www.halleonard.com/mylibrary

Enter Code
3783-8987-1132-3324

Audio Arrangements by Peter Deneff

ISBN 978-1-4950-9071-4

HAL•LEONARD®

7777 W. BLUEMOUND RD. P.O. BOX 13819 MILWAUKEE, WI 53213

In Australia Contact:
Hal Leonard Australia Pty. Ltd.
4 Lentara Court
Cheltenham, Victoria, 3192 Australia
Email: ausadmin@halleonard.com.au

Visit Hal Leonard Online at
www.halleonard.com

ALL YOU NEED IS LOVE

Horn

Words and Music by JOHN LENNON
and PAUL McCARTNEY

BLACKBIRD

Horn

Words and Music by JOHN LENNON
and PAUL McCARTNEY

DAY TRIPPER

HORN

Words and Music by JOHN LENNON
and PAUL McCARTNEY

ELEANOR RIGBY

Horn

Words and Music by JOHN LENNON
and PAUL McCARTNEY

GET BACK

HORN

Words and Music by JOHN LENNON
and PAUL McCARTNEY

HERE, THERE AND EVERYWHERE

Horn

Words and Music by JOHN LENNON
and PAUL McCARTNEY

HEY JUDE

HORN

Words and Music by JOHN LENNON
and PAUL McCARTNEY

I WILL

Horn

Words and Music by JOHN LENNON
and PAUL McCARTNEY

LET IT BE

HORN

Words and Music by JOHN LENNON
and PAUL McCARTNEY

LUCY IN THE SKY WITH DIAMONDS

Horn

Words and Music by JOHN LENNON
and PAUL McCARTNEY

OB-LA-DI, OB-LA-DA

HORN

Words and Music by JOHN LENNON
and PAUL McCARTNEY

PENNY LANE

Horn

Words and Music by JOHN LENNON
and PAUL McCARTNEY

SOMETHING

Horn

Words and Music by
GEORGE HARRISON

TICKET TO RIDE

HORN

Words and Music by JOHN LENNON
and PAUL McCARTNEY

YESTERDAY

HORN

Words and Music by JOHN LENNON
and PAUL McCARTNEY